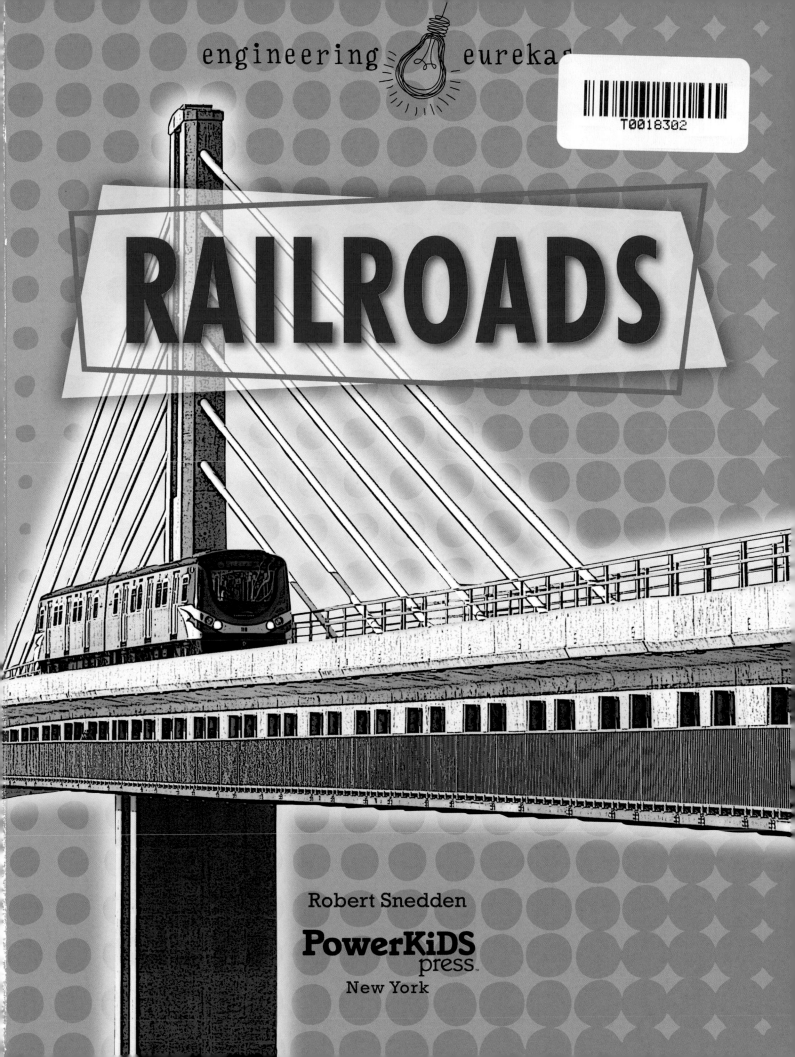

engineering eurekas

RAILROADS

Robert Snedden

PowerKiDS press
New York

Published in 2017 by

The Rosen Publishing Group, Inc.

29 East 21st Street, New York, NY 10010

Cataloging-in-Publication Data

Names: Snedden, Robert.

Title: Railroads / Robert Snedden.

Description: New York : PowerKids Press, 2017. | Series: Engineering eurekas | Includes index.

Identifiers: ISBN 9781499430974 (pbk.) | ISBN 9781499430998 (library bound) | ISBN 9781499430981 (6 pack)

Subjects: LCSH: Railroads--Juvenile literature.

Classification: LCC TF148.S64 2017 | DDC 385--dc23

Produced for Rosen by Calcium Creative Ltd

Editors for Calcium Creative Ltd: Sarah Eason and Harriet McGregor

Designers: Paul Myerscough and Jessica Moon

Picture researcher: Rachel Blount

Picture credits: Cover: Shutterstock: Iakov Filimonov. Inside: Venetia Dean 29 artwork; Shutterstock: Solodov Alexey 17r, Ananaline 6b, Paul Cowell 22–23c, Denisgo 28, Dwphotos 13r, Everett Historical 10–11, 11, FotograFFF 5r, Peter Gudella 8–9t, Jorg Hackemann 16–17t, Johnbraid 6–7, Kaband 16–17b, Konmesa 12–13, Daniel Korzeniewski 18–19, Mamahoohooba 22–23t, Meoita 9t, Modfos 1, 26–27, Scanrail1 29t, Michael G Smith 14–15, Heather Lucia Snow 3, 8–9b, Aleksandar Todorovic 21t, Ververidis Vasilis 19b, Yangchao 6–7b, Ymgerman 20–21; Wikimedia Commons: John Birkinshaw 4–5b, Cherubino 15r, Illustrated London News 18, LoKiLeCh 4–5t, Camilo Sanchez 27.

Manufactured in the United States of America

CPSIA Compliance Information: Batch #BW17PK: For Further Information contact Rosen Publishing, New York, New York at 1-800-237-9932.

Contents

Wagonways and Tracks

We take rail travel for granted these days. What is easier than jumping off and on a train? But it took a lot of engineering to get the railroads to where they are today.

Wagonways

Before the invention of railroads, wagonways were used to move goods. These were wooden tracks that were first used in Germany in the sixteenth century. Carts full of **ore** were hauled along the tracks from mines. In the eighteenth and nineteenth centuries, iron began to replace the wood on the wagonways. **Steel** then later replaced iron.

This sixteenth-century wagonway cart was used in a gold mine in Transylvania.

Captain Dick's Puffer

On December 24, 1801, British engineer Richard Trevithick (1771–1833) drove "Captain Dick's Puffer" in Cornwall, England. This was the first steam-powered, passenger-carrying road vehicle. Unfortunately, the vehicle caught fire a few days later and was destroyed.

The First Locomotive

Later, Trevithick had the idea to put a **steam engine** on rails. On February 21, 1804, his engine hauled a load of 10 tons (9 mt) of iron and 70 men for 10 miles (16 km). Trevithick built two more **locomotives** but the weight of his engines was too much for the **cast-iron** rails used at the time.

The flanges are on the rim nearest the train.

ENGINEERING FIRSTS

An important step in railroad development was the flanged wheel, which first appeared in the early seventeenth century. This is a wheel that has a rim, called a flange. It helps keep the wheel from leaving the rails.

On the Right Track

In 1820, John Birkinshaw developed a new way to make wrought iron. This meant that longer, stronger lengths of track could be laid. Then, railroads really took off.

M.ʳ JOHN BIRKINSHAW'S PATENT.

This illustration shows John Birkinshaw's new wrought iron rail track design.

Early Locomotives

George Stephenson (1781–1848) was chief mechanic at Killingworth colliery, or coal mine, in Yorkshire, England. In 1814, he built a locomotive that could haul 30 tons (27 mt) of coal at a fast walking pace.

Railroad Firsts

Stephenson's train was called the *Locomotion*. In 1825, it pulled 450 people 25 miles (40 km) from Darlington to Stockton, in England. It traveled at a speed of 15 miles (24 km) per hour. This was the world's first public passenger steam train.

By 1830, Stephenson had built a new locomotive called the *Rocket*. It was twice as fast as the *Locomotion* and provided the first regular rail passenger service on the Liverpool and Manchester Railway in Lancashire, England.

PETER

ENGINEERING FIRSTS

Stephenson's vision of a network of standard railroad lines became a reality.

Stephenson designed cast-iron edge rails on the tracks. This was to keep the tracks from breaking as heavy locomotives passed over them. His rail **gauge** of 4 feet 8.5 inches (1.435 m) is the standard gauge for most of the world's railroads today. It is sometimes called "Stephenson gauge."

Stephenson's orginal Locomotion no longer exists. This is a carefully reconstructed full-sized replica.

Engineers did not think a locomotive could run over hilly tracks but Cooper proved them wrong.

Tom Thumb

Early locomotives were known as "iron horses." The first one to run in the United States was the *Stourbridge Lion*. This was shipped from the United Kingdom to New York City in 1829. Unfortunately, it was too heavy for the tracks it ran on.

The first steam locomotive built in the United States was the *Tom Thumb*. It was designed by engineer and inventor Peter Cooper (1791–1833). Cooper believed he could build a locomotive that would handle the hilly and twisting route planned for the new Baltimore and Ohio Railroad Company. By 1830, his small-but-powerful *Tom Thumb* was ready. The locomotive was put together from a mix of parts, including old musket (gun) barrels! However, the demonstration was a success for steam power.

Steam Power

A steam locomotive is a steam engine that goes places. The energy source for the first steam engines was usually coal, which was burned to boil water. This produced steam, which powered the engine.

How a Steam Engine Works

The boiler of a locomotive holds water. The firebox is where the coal is burned. Metal tubes carry heat from the firebox to the boiler. This boils the water, producing steam. The steam is directed through an inlet **valve** into a cylinder, where it pushes down on a **piston**. There are two cylinders, one on each side of the locomotive. The piston moves a crank and connecting rod. These are attached to one or more of the locomotive's wheels. The piston's movements turn the wheels, driving them along the track.

As the locomotive moves, the crank pushes the piston back up the cylinder. The inlet valve closes and an outlet valve opens, allowing the steam to escape out of the locomotive's chimney. Then the inlet valve opens once more, and the whole cycle starts again.

The crank and connecting rods are turning this steam locomotive's wheels.

The Rocket had four wheels and pulled its water tank behind it.

ENGINEERING FIRSTS

George Stephenson's *Rocket* was one of the first locomotives to use many tubes to heat its boiler. These were much more efficient than the design of a single tube surrounded by water that had been used before. The tubes helped the engine produce more power.

Boiler Pressure

It was particularly important that the boiler was strong enough to hold the high-pressure steam inside. If the pressure (pushing force) got too high, the boiler could, and sometimes did, explode! In 1856, John Ramsbottom (1814–1897) invented a safety valve that was then used on all locomotives.

The Union Pacific "Big Boy" was one of the largest ever steam locomotives.

Rails Across the Nation

In the mid-nineteenth century, crossing the United States meant traveling on horseback or by horse-drawn wagon. People traveled over mountains, deserts, and plains on a dangerous journey that could take five months or more. That was soon to change.

Across the United States

In 1862, President Abraham Lincoln (1809–1865) authorized the building of a railroad to cross the United States. It was called the Transcontinental Railroad. Work started in 1863. The Central Pacific Railroad company built east from Sacramento, California. The Union Pacific company built west from Council Bluffs, Iowa. The distance to be crossed was 1,907 miles (3,069 km).

The railroad engineers cut a path through the Sierra Nevada Mountains in California called the Bloomer Cut.

Summit Tunnel

The Central Pacific dug tunnels through the Sierra Nevada Mountains. The Summit Tunnel through the Donner Pass was one of the most challenging of all. Construction crews started from east and west. Two more crews dug down from above to take debris, or loose material, out of the tunnel. It took almost two years to dig the tunnel. Sometimes, it took a whole day just to get through 1 foot (30 cm) of rock.

The people who planned the route of the Summit Tunnel were incredibly accurate. Having drilled and blasted through more than 1,600 feet (500 m) of rock, the teams were only a few inches off when the crews working from east and west met.

A ceremony was held as the last spike was hammered in.

ENGINEERING FIRSTS

The two lines built by the Central Pacific and Union Pacific met on May 10, 1869, at Promontory, Utah. Other lines were linked into this Transcontinental Railroad. On June 4, 1876, the *Transcontinental Express* arrived in San Francisco only 83 hours and 39 minutes after it had left New York City. It was the first locomotive to make the coast-to-coast journey.

Laying Track

The railroads of Europe, where the population is dense, were built for heavy-duty use. They had few slopes and bends and often had multiple tracks. In North and South America, towns are more widely separated and the railroads were of lighter construction.

Gauge

The track gauge can affect the cost of building a railroad. Locomotives that run on narrow gauges are usually smaller and cheaper. These are often used in less wealthy countries or countries with smaller populations.

Roadbed

Before a track can be laid, a **roadbed**, or trackbed, is dug out so the rails have a flat, stable surface to rest on. Modern earth-moving equipment has made this a lot easier than in the early days of railroads, when this work was done by hand. The track is fastened to **crossties**, or **sleepers**, to keep them spaced correctly. These are embedded in a tightly packed foundation, or base, of crushed rock. The busier the track, the deeper the foundation.

Modern Rail

British engineer Charles Vignoles (1793–1875) invented the modern railroad rail. This rail has a flat base and is a little like an upside down "T" in shape. Rails used today are still very similar to Vignoles' invention. However, modern steel means that rails are now hardier and longer lasting.

Skilled welders join the railroad tracks smoothly together.

ENGINEERING FIRSTS

One of the most important developments in railroad construction was the **welding** together of standard 100-foot-long (30-m) rails into lengths of between 950 and 1,300 feet (290 and 400 m). Once laid, these long lengths can be welded together to form unbroken rail lines several miles long. Welded rails were first tried in the United States in 1933. They are now used throughout the world's major rail networks.

The wooden crossties are embedded in the roadbed.

Diesel Power

A big change came to the railroads with the appearance of the first **diesel**-powered locomotives. In the 1920s, several countries began working on **prototype** diesels. By the 1940s, diesels were built that could rival any steam locomotive. As they were less expensive to operate, they soon began to take over from steam locomotives. They replaced steam almost entirely by the 1960s.

Advantages of Diesel

The diesel locomotive was much more reliable than steam and could operate for longer periods without servicing. Diesels were four times more efficient than steam locomotives because they needed a lot less fuel. This made them much less expensive to run. Diesels also had faster, smoother **acceleration**. They could travel faster for longer and caused less wear on tracks.

Built in the 1950s, this diesel locomotive was used to pull passenger carriages in the United States.

Diesel-Electric

Most diesels do not drive the wheels directly from the diesel engine. Instead, the diesel is used to power an electric **generator**. The generator produces the electricity needed to drive electric motors and power the locomotive. Diesel-mechanical locomotives are powered directly by the diesel engine. These trains are mostly used for slow **shunting** work and not for freight or passenger services.

ENGINEERING FIRSTS

The Fliegender Hamburger is ready to set off.

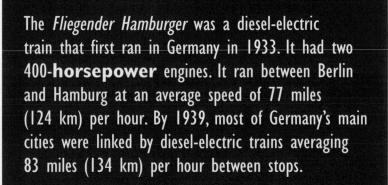

The *Fliegender Hamburger* was a diesel-electric train that first ran in Germany in 1933. It had two 400-**horsepower** engines. It ran between Berlin and Hamburg at an average speed of 77 miles (124 km) per hour. By 1939, most of Germany's main cities were linked by diesel-electric trains averaging 83 miles (134 km) per hour between stops.

Electrifying the Railroad

People first used electric batteries to power locomotives as early as 1835. One of the first countries to electrify an entire railroad line was Italy, in 1902.

In Europe today, high-speed electric trains connect cities.

Electric Expansion

Through the twentieth century, electrified railroads were built all over the world. By the end of the 1920s, every country in Europe had some electrified track. In the United States, the first electric locomotive for use on standard gauge rail tracks ran in New York State in 1883. However, very little of the US rail network has been electrified and most of that is in the Boston-Washington, DC area.

These trucks are adapted to run on rails when they repair overhead power lines.

Power Points

Electric locomotives are **economical** and efficient, as long as there is a reliable source of electricity. They are also quieter and cleaner as they do not produce smoke or fumes. Power is transmitted to the train through either an overhead wire or at ground level using a third rail laid close to the main rails. Overhead systems use a collector called a **pantograph**. This is attached to the roof of the train and keeps it in contact with the power supply.

The first electric train could carry passengers.

ENGINEERING FIRSTS

The first successful electric locomotive ran at an exhibition in Berlin in 1879. The world's first public electric railroad opened near Berlin in 1881. It was soon followed by more.

Power Failure

One disadvantage of electric locomotives is that they have no engine. They depend completely on the power from the overhead cables or electrified rail. If there is any interruption to the power supply, the train stops.

Going Underground

Many of the world's major cities, including New York City, London, Paris, and Moscow, have an underground subway system. These form part of the **metro**, or **rapid transit** system. They would not have been possible without electric locomotives. Imagine how smoke-filled the tunnels would have become.

ENGINEERING FIRSTS

The City and South London Railway was the first fully underground, electric-powered rapid transit railroad. It opened in 1890. Today, it is part of the London Underground system.

Moscow's Mayakovskaya metro station is built 100 feet (33 m) below ground.

When it opened, the City and South London line had just six stations.

Rubber-Tired Trains

Some underground systems use trains with rubber tires. They run on concrete or steel **rollways** and are quieter than trains with steel wheels. Montreal and Paris both have rubber-tired trains as part of their metro systems.

Cut and Cover

There are different methods for digging subway tunnels. The cut and cover method involves digging a deep trench in the city streets and constructing a tunnel inside it. The trench is then filled in and the roadway rebuilt. This causes huge disruption to traffic and gas pipes and sewers often need to be rerouted. This method is used in the Paris Metro and the New York City Subway.

Boring Tunnels

An alternative method is to bore the tunnels. Workers sink a vertical shaft into the ground from which the tunnels are dug out horizontally. The advantage of this is that it avoids disruption to the streets above. The downside is that tunneling is much more expensive than cut and cover. It might require blasting to get through any areas of solid rock. Specialized tunnel-boring machines can sometimes be used as an alternative to blasting.

This tunnel-boring equipment is being used to cut a tunnel for the metro in Thessaloniki, Greece.

The Search for Speed

High-speed trains travel at 155 miles (250 km) per hour or more on new tracks and at 125 miles (200 km) per hour or more on older tracks. Many countries now have high-speed rail links connecting their major cities.

Around the Bend

The faster a train travels, the longer the bends and curves must be in the track. High-speed trains run on standard gauge tracks welded together into longer lengths. This keeps the vibrations, or shaking movements, from building up and causing a derailment.

Making It Better

On April 20, 1959, work began on the first stretch of track for a new high-speed rail system in Japan. Five years later, in October 1964, the first modern high-speed rail opened. It was called the Tokaido Shinkansen.

This Chinese Railway high-speed train has a long, pointed nose to help it speed quickly through the air.

ENGINEERING FIRSTS

The Shinkansen passing through Tokyo.

By 1976, the number of passengers carried on the Tokaido Shinkansen had reached 1 billion. Since it opened, Japan's rail engineers have increased speeds. They have also reduced the noise the train makes as it enters a tunnel and reduced vibration. They have also reduced the braking distance and improved the energy efficiency.

The Tokaido Shinkansen ran between Tokyo and Osaka and could cover a distance of 320 miles (515 km) in just 3 hours and 10 minutes.

World's Fastest Rail Service

The fastest high-speed rail service in the world today is the Shanghai maglev, which began in 2004. It has a maximum speed of 270 miles (430 km) per hour and an average speed of 156 miles (251 km) per hour.

Maglev Magic

Maglev means "magnetic **levitation**." These trains use the **repelling** force of powerful magnets to lift the train clear of the tracks. Maglev trains give a very smooth high-speed ride.

How Is It Done?

If you have ever played with magnets, you will know that if you point them toward each other in the right way they push apart. This is the principle behind the maglev train. A magnetized coil runs along the trackway and repels large magnets on the underside of the train. The magnets lift the train up to 4 inches (10 cm) above the trackway. Once the train has levitated, the electric current in the trackway coil is quickly switched back and forth. The result of this is that the magnetic force in front of the train pulls it along and at the same time the force behind the train pushes it forward.

The Chinese high-speed Shanghai maglev carries passengers along this trackway from Pudong International Airport to Longyang Road Station.

The sides of this maglev curve around the trackway.

Friction Free

Because the maglev train floats on a cushion of air, there is no **friction** between the train and the trackway to slow it down. All that slows it is air resistance, called drag. This is the force of the air on the train. The train is shaped to cut drag down to a minimum. The result is speed. In 2015, an experimental Japanese maglev hit an incredible 374 miles (603 km) per hour.

FUTURE EUREKAS!

In Japan, there are plans to introduce a maglev service between Tokyo and the city of Nagoya by 2027. The service would run at a top speed of 310 miles (500 km) per hour. However, estimates for the construction costs stand at nearly $100 billion.

Global Railroads

Seattle to Los Angeles: 1,378 miles (2,216 km), journey time 35 hours

Emeryville, California, to Chicago, Illinois: 2,438 miles (3,924 km), journey time 52 hours

Toronto to Vancouver, Canada: 2,775 miles (4,466 km), journey time 86 hours

EUROPE

NORTH AMERICA

SOUTH AMERICA

What advantages do you think there are in transporting goods by railroad instead of by road?

In terms of safety, how do you think railroad travel might compare with road or air travel?

What ways can you think of to improve the railroad network where you live?

Moscow to Vladivostok, Russia: 5,750 miles (9,259 km), journey time 178 hours

Moscow, Russia, to Beijing, China: 5,582 miles (8,984 km), journey time 144 hours

ASIA

Qinghai, China, to Lhasa, Tibet: 2,700 miles (4,345 km), journey time 51 hours

Dibrugarh to Kanyakumari, India: 2,665 miles (4,286 km), journey time 83 hours

AFRICA

Adelaide to Darwin, Australia: 1,850 miles (2,980 km), journey time 50 hours

Do you think it is a good idea for major cities to have a rapid transit, metro rail service? Why?

AUSTRALIA

Pretoria to Cape Town, South Africa: 994 miles (1,600 km), journey time 27 hours

Fast Forward

What shape could the railroads of the future take? How about trains that drive themselves? Or maybe there will be trains traveling at almost the speed of sound!

Driverless Trains

Trains that do not have a human driver but have a human to start them and open the doors are common across the world. More than 30 cities, including New York City and London, have at least some semiautomatic train lines. There are also trains that operate completely free of human controllers. The Vancouver and Copenhagen metro systems are like this. Honolulu plans to open the United States' first driverless transportation system in 2018.

Vancouver's Skytrain is the world's oldest fully automated rapid transit system.

Hyperloop

Hyperloop is an idea for a very fast transport system linking major cities at speeds faster than the speed of sound. It was proposed by businessman Elon Musk in 2013. It would work in a similar way to a maglev. However, instead of traveling in the open air, it would move along a tube from which most of the air had been removed. By reducing air resistance, the train should reach speeds of around 760 miles (1,200 km) per hour!

The original plan was for the Hyperloop to link San Francisco and Los Angeles, California. However, the Slovakian government is also looking into building a Hyperloop network.

The Hyperloop would be almost frictionless. It would only need to use energy to accelerate at the start of the journey and decelerate at the end. In between, it could just glide.

If they are built, the Hyperloop tunnels may be aboveground rather than underground.

Here to Stay

So what will happen to railroads in the future? There is no doubt that they will continue to exist for as far ahead as we can see. But will they exist in the same form as they do now?

A Driverless Railroad

The use of driverless trains might become even more widespread. Sensors embedded in the track could send signals to driverless trains to tell them whether or not the track is busy. They would tell them when to slow down and when it is safe to hit top speed.

FUTURE EUREKAS!

In the future, squads of robots may take over the task of laying new track. The robots would also monitor the state of the existing track and carry out repairs as necessary. Rail operators would keep an eye on progress using drones.

Could a future railroad run high above city streets?

A Railroad Future

At the moment, railroads are the best way to transport large amounts of freight across land. They also provide a convenient urban transportation system for people in our cities. As long as we have a need to move people and our goods from one place to another, railroads are here to stay.

Be an Engineer

See for yourself how a maglev train works!

You Will Need:
- A pencil
- Two or more ring magnets that will fit onto the pencil

- Hold the pencil upright and slide the first ring magnet onto it.
- Place your second magnet on top of the first. If the magnets attract one another, take the second one off and reverse its direction.
- What happens now? If the two magnets repel each other, the second will float above the first.
- Try adding more magnets and see what happens!

Glossary

acceleration The rate at which something changes speed.

cast iron A hard but brittle type of iron.

crossties The supports for the rails in a railroad track, laid at right angles to the track.

diesel A liquid fuel, often made from petroleum.

economical Good value for the money spent.

friction A force that slows down or keeps objects from moving against each other.

gauge The spacing between the rails on a railroad, measured from the inner faces of the rails.

generator A machine that turns mechanical energy into electricity.

horsepower A measure of an engine's power.

levitation The act of rising and hovering in the air.

locomotives Powered railroad vehicles, used for pulling trains.

metro An underground railroad system in a city.

ore Rock from which metals can be extracted.

pantograph A framework that supplies electricity to a train from an overhead line.

piston A cylinder that moves up and down.

prototype The first version of a machine or vehicle from which others will be developed.

rapid transit A transportation system usually equipped to quickly move large numbers of passengers in cities.

repelling Pushing away.

roadbed The material on which the rails and crossties rest.

rollways Surfaces along which things can be rolled.

shunting Pushing or pulling another train.

sleepers The supports for the rails in a railroad track, laid at right angles to the track.

steam engine An engine that uses steam to produce power.

steel A strong metal made from iron and carbon.

valve A device that controls the movement of a gas or liquid.

welding Joining together two pieces of metal using heat.

Further Reading

Books

Farndon, John. *Stickmen's Guide to Trains and Automobiles* (Stickmen's Guides to How Everything Works). Minneapolis, MN: Hungry Tomato, 2016.

Floca, Brian. *Locomotive*. New York, NY: Atheneum, 2013.

Train: The Definitive Visual History (DK Smithsonian). New York, NY: Dorling Kindersley, 2015.

Sandler, Martin W. *Iron Rails, Iron Men.* Somerville, MA: Candlewick Press, 2015.

Websites

Due to the changing nature of Internet links, PowerKids Press has developed an online list of websites related to the subject of this book. This site is updated regularly. Please use this link to access the list:

www.powerkidslinks.com/ee/rail

Index